SPOOKED!

MYSTERIOUS DISAPPEARANCES

INVESTIGATING HISTORY'S MYSTERIES

Louise Spilsbury

CHERITON

CHILDREN'S BOOKS

Published in 2024 by **Cheriton Children's Books**
1 Bank Drive West, Shrewsbury, Shropshire, SY3 9DJ, UK

© 2024 Cheriton Children's Books

First Edition

Author: Louise Spilsbury
Designer: Jessica Moon
Editor: Jennifer Sanderson
Proofreader: Ella Hammond

Picture credits: Cover: Shutterstock/Fotokita (fg), Shutterstock/Alvov (bg). Inside: p1: Shutterstock/Wirestock Creators, p4b: Shutterstock/Muratart, p4c: Shutterstock/Carlos Criado, p5: Shutterstock/Raggedstone, p6bl: Shutterstock/Paulina Goral, p6br: Wikimedia Commons/Sir John Everett Millais/Royal Holloway Art & Culture, p7: Shutterstock/Everett Collection, p8: Shutterstock/Meunierd, p9: Shutterstock/Nong2, p10: Wikimedia Commons/Frank S. Davis, p11tl: Shutterstock/Muratart, p11tr: Shutterstock/Sergey Nivens, p12: Shutterstock/Olesia Bilkei, p13: Shutterstock/Tomas Kotouc, p14bl: Shutterstock/Kim Hefner, p14br: Wikimedia Commons/Daniel Candido, p15: Shutterstock/wee dezign, p16bl: Shutterstock/Marcelo Treichel Vianna, p16br: Shutterstock/Reeh, p17: Wikimedia Commons/Michael Kan, p18bl: Shutterstock/Erlantz P R, p18br: Shutterstock/Zef Art, p19: Shutterstock/Kiselev Andrey Valerevich, p20b: Shutterstock/Zef Art, p20c: Shutterstock/Fotokita, p21: Shutterstock/Muratart, p22: Shutterstock/Iobard, p23: Wikimedia Commons/US Navy/Sargent, p24: Shutterstock/Aastels, p25c: Shutterstock/Fotokita, p25t: Shutterstock/Elena Dijour, p26b: Shutterstock/Sagittarius Pro, p26c: Shutterstock/New Africa, p27: Shutterstock/Zef Art, p28: Shutterstock/Pedal to the Stock, p29: Shutterstock/Muhammad Amirul Azmi, p30: Shutterstock/Wirestock Creators, p31: Shutterstock/Everett Collection, p33b: Shutterstock/Evgeniyqw, p33t: Shutterstock/Mishainik, p34: Shutterstock/Katarzyna Klimasz, p35: Shutterstock/PomInOz, p36: Shutterstock/Arlene Waller, p37: Shutterstock/Kamomeen, p39: Shutterstock/Denis Andricic, p40: Shutterstock/Fer Gregory, p41: Shutterstock/Breakermaximus, p42: Shutterstock/Muratinan, p44bl: Shutterstock/Denis Belitsky, p44br: Shutterstock/Torwaistudio, p45: Wikimedia Commons/William Ludwell Sheppard/William James Linton.

Printed in China

Please visit our website,
www.cheritonchildrensbooks.com
to see more of our high-quality books.

CONTENTS

CHAPTER 1

VANISHED WITHOUT A TRACE

Can people really disappear into thin air? There is something very spooky about reports of people vanishing without a trace but there have been mysterious disappearances like this throughout history. These strange cases have never been solved.

Lost Forever?

Some people left home and never made it to their destination. Others may have been kidnapped, or taken, or murdered, and their bodies never discovered. These disappearances happened in different places and times, to people of different ages and from different backgrounds. A common factor in many is that while there are theories, or ideas, about what happened, no one really knows the truth.

Stolen by the Sky?

One of the oldest mysterious disappearances took place in Rome, Italy, in the eighth century BCE. **Legend** has it that Romulus, a son of the Roman god Mars, killed his twin brother Remus, so that he could rule the city of Rome on his own. Rome was named for him, and under his leadership, it became very rich and powerful. Then, after almost 40 years in power, Romulus vanished without a trace! The Roman **historian** Livy said Romulus was inspecting troops when he disappeared during a sudden and violent storm.

A writer named Plutarch said that Romulus disappeared during a solar eclipse when the Moon blocked the Sun and everything went dark.

Throughout history, hundreds of people have vanished without a trace.

Was He Stabbed?

Was Romulus stabbed to death under the cover of darkness? Some Romans believed that senators, the men who made up Rome's government, killed Romulus so they could take control. They said that the senators murdered Romulus when darkness suddenly fell. Then they cut his body into pieces that they could hide under their robes, and secretly carried them from the crime scene.

Gone to the Gods?

Some Romans believed that Romulus had not died at all. They claimed that he was really a god named Quirinus who visited Earth to help the Romans create a great **empire**. Some said they saw Romulus wearing brightly shining armor and going up into the sky, as if to join the gods. Some Romans questioned whether Romulus was even a real person. If he was, how did he vanish without a trace?

SET TO SPOOK!

In this book, we are going to explore some of the most unsettling reports about mysterious disappearances. You'll hear about missing people who are thought to be dead, people who seemed to vanish in thin air, and cases where entire communities were lost forever. Some of the stories will send shivers down your spine. Some of them will leave you truly spooked!

Missing Monarchs

Being rich and famous or even belonging to royalty seems to provide no protection from the risk of mysteriously vanishing. In fact, it seems to increase the chances of being lost in the mists of time.

Terror in the Tower

The disappearance of two young English princes in 1483 is one of the spookiest mysteries in history. Prince Edward was just 12 years old when his father King Edward IV died in 1483. Prince Edward became King Edward V, but his uncle, Richard, Duke of Gloucester, took charge of the country, supposedly just until Edward was old enough to rule. However, the Duke sent Edward and his brother Prince Richard to the Tower of London in England. They were never seen again and the Duke of Gloucester declared himself king. Many people suspected the princes had been murdered but no bodies were found.

SPOOKED!

In 1674, a wooden chest containing two small skeletons was discovered buried beneath an old staircase in the Tower of London. Pieces of velvet were on the bones. At the time, only royals wore velvet, suggesting that the bones were the princes'. Examination of the bones in the 1930s confirmed they were from two young people of the same age as the princes but, as yet, there is no definite proof that the bones belong to them.

The young princes trapped in the Tower of London must have been terrified.

The Romanov family was
murdered (see below),
but not all of the bodies
were found...

Shot or Survived?

It is not only princes who suddenly disappear. Princess Anastasia Romanov was the youngest daughter of the Russian ruler **Tsar** Nicolas II. In 1917, **rebels** took power from the tsar and in 1918, it was reported that the Romanov family had all been shot dead. But stories that Anastasia had escaped began immediately and lasted for many years. Several people claimed to be her. In 1920, a woman named Anna Anderson claimed she was Anastasia. Anderson said she had survived the shooting because bullets fired at her had hit jewels hidden in her clothing. Anderson stuck to her story until her death in 1984. After her death, **DNA** tests proved she was not Anastasia but an imposter, or a person pretending to be someone else.

A Gruesome Discovery

Remains of the Romanov family's bodies were found and dug up in 1991 but there was still no sign of Anastasia, so people believed that she really had survived. Then, in 2007, the burned remains of two bodies were found near the original remains. DNA tests confirmed that this was the final resting place of Anastasia and her brother Alexei.

MISSING OUTLAWS

Spooky Shoot-Outs

Butch Cassidy and his partner in crime, the Sundance Kid, were leaders of the Wild Bunch. The Wild Bunch was a gang that held up banks and robbed trains in the Rocky Mountains in the 1890s. The official version of Cassidy and the Kid's disappearance is that soldiers gunned them down. However, many people believe that Cassidy escaped and lived for decades under a secret identity.

The Wild Bunch

Butch Cassidy was born Robert LeRoy Parker. He took "Cassidy" from a cattle **rustler** he met, and was nicknamed "Butch" after working in a butcher's store. Cassidy met the Sundance Kid in 1896. As leaders of the Wild Bunch, Cassidy and the Sundance Kid made sure the gang was very well organized. They carefully planned escape routes in advance of each robbery and used fresh horses to ensure quick getaways. Angry at being outsmarted and robbed, railroad bosses and bank owners sent numerous investigators to hunt down the gang.

On the Run

Tired of constantly being on the run, in 1901, Cassidy and the Sundance Kid bought a ranch in Argentina, South America, under fake names. Then, in 1908, Cassidy and Sundance were accused of stealing wages being delivered by a mining company's courier in Bolivia, South America. Soldiers tracked them to a house nearby and there was a shoot-out.

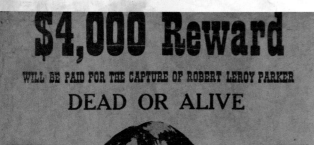

Wanted posters of the two outlaws were posted throughout the Wild West.

Butch Cassidy is part of Wild West legend. Was he killed in a shoot-out or did he have another, secret, life?

Dead and Buried?

The soldiers reported hearing two shots from inside the house and two men were found dead inside. The courier identified the bodies as Butch and Sundance. Yet, he also admitted that the outlaws were wearing masks during the robbery. No photographs of the bodies were taken to provide proof, and they were quickly buried nearby.

The Plot Thickens

Some people believe that Cassidy had not died. Back in the United States, over the years there were more than 20 well-documented sightings of him. His sister Lula said that in 1925 Butch visited his family, driving a shiny new Ford. She claimed that he kept in touch with them until he died from **pneumonia** in 1937. His burial site has remained a secret because his family said that Butch was chased all his life and finally, he had a chance to rest in peace.

Solving the Case

People have tried to solve the mystery of Cassidy for many years. One theory is that a friend of Cassidy planted the story of his death in Bolivia so that law enforcement agents would no longer chase him. In the early 1990s, two bodies believed to be the outlaws were dug up. DNA tests proved they were not Cassidy and Sundance. To this day, the mystery of the legendary outlaw Butch Cassidy remains unsolved.

CHAPTER 2

EXPLORERS GO MISSING

There was a time when much of the world was still unknown to people. Even today, there are parts of the thickest rain forests, widest deserts, or highest mountains where few, if any, people have ever been. There are brave and curious adventurers who set out to discover the deepest, darkest corners of the world. These explorers often face great danger and many who set out on great **expeditions** vanish without a trace.

Two Brothers, Two Disappearances

In a chilling coincidence, Portuguese brothers Gaspar and Miguel Corte-Real disappeared during separate voyages to the coastline of modern-day Canada. In 1501, three ships, including one carrying Gaspar, visited the coast and captured slaves. But, only two ships made it out of the area: Gaspar and his ship went missing. When Miguel heard that his brother had vanished, he set out to rescue him the following year. But, he vanished too. What became of the two brothers remains a mystery.

Did Miguel make the markings on Dighton Rock?

SPOOKED!

Some people claim that the curious carvings on the Dighton Rock in Berkley, Massachusetts, are a message that Miguel wrote. They claim that the lines and shapes on the rock say Miguel became a chief of the Native Americans who once lived there.

Sailing in the rough Arctic waters was especially dangerous during the 1600s.

A Risky Route

Several explorers lost their lives or went missing while searching for a sea route between the Atlantic and Pacific Oceans, which is now known as the Northwest Passage. Explorers were determined to find this ice-free area because it would mean a shorter shipping route for ships traveling between Europe and Asia. Different attempts to find the passage had already claimed many lives when English explorer Henry Hudson and his crew set sail on the *Discovery* in 1610.

Cast Adrift

Hudson and his crew sailed across the Atlantic to northern Canada but soon found themselves trapped by icy waters in a bay. There was no escaping the Arctic winter. It was freezing and the crew became angry with Hudson. By June 1611, the *Discovery* was free of ice and could leave the bay but, by then, the crew were furious that they had wasted their time and risked their lives. They turned against Hudson and set him and eight others adrift in a small rowing boat. They were never seen again. What happened to them remains a mystery.

Many adventurers disappeared in the cold and icy conditions of the Arctic.

More Unsolved Mysteries

Nineteenth-century explorers took daring risks and faced incredible hardships. Some ventured across icy seas into the coldest places on the planet. Others traveled into some of the most **remote** and driest deserts on Earth.

A Time of Terror

In 1845, the aptly named HMS *Terror* and another ship set out with 129 men on an Arctic expedition. By 1848, the ships had been stuck in Arctic ice for nearly two years. Fierce winds and blizzards blasted the two ships, and ice threatened to crush them. It was freezing cold and the crew was starving.

On April 22, 1848, the captain of the *Terror*, Francis Crozier, decided to abandon ship. He and the crew set off on foot, hoping to find a fur hunters' camp. It was their final trip—they were never seen again.

A Haunting Tale

What happened to Crozier and his men remains a mystery. Local **Inuit** people told search parties they had seen piles of human bones, cracked in half. This may suggest that Crozier's crew ate the flesh of men who died and cracked their bones to eat the **marrow** inside. Some bodies have been found frozen in the ice but not all. The body of Francis Crozier himself was never discovered.

A Risky Plan

German explorer Ludwig Leichhardt was already famous for his explorations of Australia when he set out on his fourth expedition in 1848. He planned to travel on horseback east-to-west across Australia through its loneliest, driest deserts. He set out in March 1848 and was last seen on April 3. Leichhardt and the 7 men, 20 mules, 50 bullocks, and 7 horses with him disappeared.

Dead in the Desert?

Searches for Leichhardt began in 1852 and continued into the 1930s. For years, nothing at all was found. In 1900, a brass plaque attached to a gun, with Leichhardt's name and dated 1848, was found wedged in a tree. A letter "L" was carved into the tree, something Leichhardt was known to do along his routes. This suggests he made it two-thirds of the way across Australia but his disappearance remains a mystery.

SPOOKED!

There are several spooky theories about Leichhardt's end. Were he and his team murdered? Did his team turn on him and kill him? Did he live with **Aboriginal** people in the middle of the desert? Perhaps the team starved or drowned. One theory is that a shark ate Leichhardt in the waters of the Gulf of Carpentaria, which is a large, shallow sea in northern Australia.

Maybe a shark killed and ate Leichhardt in the dangerous waters of the Gulf of Carpentaria?

Rain Forest Mysteries

Rain forests are some of the most beautiful places on Earth but they can also be deadly. It is easy for people to lose their way in these thick, tangled forests where dangerous wild animals lurk and poisonous plants grow. Some explorers who entered the deepest, darkest rain forests never returned.

Searching for a Lost City

British explorer Colonel Percy Fawcett was obsessed with finding a mysterious lost city, which he named Z, in the Amazon rain forest. In 1925, Fawcett, his son, and an explorer named Raleigh Rimmell set off deep into the rain forest. Fawcett's last known letter was written on May 29, 1925, at Dead Horse Camp. In it he said they were heading into unexplored land. The three men were never seen again.

More Vanish

Since 1925, many expeditions have searched for the truth of Fawcett's disappearance. Some of these search parties also vanished without a trace. In spite of finding some of Fawcett's belongings, such as a ring and his compass, no one really knows what happened. Some believe that the men were killed by cannibals, people who eat human flesh. Others think they became lost and starved to death.

Maybe we will never know the truth about what happened to Percy Fawcett...

There are many stories about what had happened to the missing rain forest girl (see below). Some said rain forest spirits had saved her, while others say a strange wild man had been seen with her. Perhaps he had cared for her in the rain forest?

Might there be a spooky explanation for what happened to the missing girl?

Swallowed by the Forest

The rain forest still claims victims, today. In 2007, a mystery woman emerged from the rain forest in Cambodia, Asia. She was starving and could not speak. A man claimed that the rain forest girl was his daughter who went missing while tending a herd of buffalo in 1988. She was just eight years old when she disappeared. The rain forest girl stayed with the family but she often tried to escape to the rain forest and it became clear that she had mental health problems. Perhaps, her difficult time alone in the wild rain forest caused them?

Lost in the Rain Forest

In 2016, there was another twist in the tale. A family from across the border in Vietnam arrived in the village. They claimed that the rain forest girl was their missing daughter Tak, who had disappeared from home in 2006. Tak vanished at the age of 23 after having a mental breakdown. Officials spent two weeks reviewing the case and in August 2016, the woman was returned to her real family in Vietnam. The mystery remains. If the so-called rain forest girl is Tak, what happened to the young girl who vanished in 1989?

THE LOP DESERT

Peng Sets Off

In June 1980, a well-known Chinese scientist named Peng Jiamu walked into the Lop Desert in China and disappeared forever. Peng was following his dream to explore some of the wildest reaches of China. His strange vanishing still haunts adventurers and scientists today.

Will the fate of Peng Jiamu remain an unsolved mystery of the sands?

A Lonely Location

The area around the Lop Desert was a salt lake 1,000 years ago. Salt lakes contain potash, which is used as fertilizer, or plant food. Lop is a vast and lonely sea of dry sand that is often blasted by violent winds. It is also dotted with ancient burial grounds and mysteries. Nonetheless, Peng and his team set out to study the levels of potash in this remote desert.

The harsh Lop Desert soon turns bodies into dried remains. One of the most famous mummies of the Lop area is the Princess of Xiaohe, who was buried around 3,800 years ago.

A Doomed Mission

The expedition hit problems early on. Peng and his team's vehicles kept sinking into the moving sand. The team started running out of food, water, and gasoline. The rest of the team gave up and called the army to rescue them but Peng refused to give up. He sneaked away, leaving a note saying he had gone to find water. After the rescue helicopters arrived, a search was launched but, apart from a candy wrapper and some footprints, there was no sign of Peng.

Spooky Speculations

There were four more full-scale searches but no trace of Peng was found. Some people speculated, or guessed, that Americans had kidnapped him or that he fled to Russia. Others believed aliens had taken him from the spooky desert, which they thought had strange powers. One person even claimed to have seen him in a Washington D.C. restaurant. Expedition organizer, Xia Xuncheng said Peng either got lost in the high winds that fateful night or had been buried under a ridge of sand that collapsed onto him and been moved far away by shifting dunes.

Murmurings of Murder...

Over the years, several **mummified** remains and skeletons have been dug up in the Lop area but DNA tests showed no match with Peng. One of the bodies was reported to have stab wounds. Some of Peng's teammates later complained he was stubborn and bad tempered. If they killed Peng to stop him forcing the expedition to go on in dangerous conditions, could the Chinese government have covered this up, and if so, why?

CHAPTER 3

LOST AT SEA

The oceans cover almost three-quarters of our planet but most of us are in the dark about what it's like out there in the deep sea and just how spooky oceans can be.

Threats at Sea

In some places in the ocean, pirates are often on the lookout for tourist boats and yachts. These vessels have little protection and they often have valuables aboard. Sometimes, the people on them are kidnapped and held for **ransom**, murdered, or simply thrown overboard. Ships can sink and people can be tossed overboard by wild weather, from dangerous hurricanes to giant thundering waves called tsunamis. There are also the threats of floating icebergs that can snap a ship in two and powerful ocean currents that can drag people far away. No wonder the oceans of the world cause so many spooky and mysterious disappearances.

Cape Fear

On New Year's Eve in 1812, Theodosia Burr Alston had boarded a ship in South Carolina bound for New York City. She, a friend, and the ship's small crew were never seen again. However, people claim to have seen the terrifying sight of the ghost of Theodosia being chased by three ghostly pirates on an island in Cape Fear.

The sea can be a dangerous and deadly place.

Some places are named for the real dangers they cause. For example, Cape Fear in North Carolina was so-named because sailors feared their ships would be wrecked on this long **headland**. And the Devil's Sea is an area of the Pacific Ocean near Japan, Asia, that is said to make people disappear through mysterious forces.

What happened to Theodosia at Cape Fear?

A Troubled Family

Theodosia was saddened after losing her only child to a deadly disease. She was heading to New York City to see her beloved father Aaron Burr. Burr had his own troubles. He had been vice president of the United States but had fallen out of favor since killing the popular Alexander Hamilton in a fight. Burr died never knowing what had become of his dear daughter.

A Mysterious End

Some say Theodosia's ship sank during a storm or that it crashed into the deadly Frying Pan Shoals, a **sandbar** off Cape Fear. A more chilling theory is that pirates waved lanterns along the shore of Cape Fear. The captain thought the lights were from another boat and that it was safe to sail there. When Theodosia's ship crashed on the sandbar, the pirates robbed and killed them. Does this explain why Theodosia's ghost is said to haunt those shores to this very day?

A Ghost Ship

The oceans hold the secrets to many unsolved mysteries. On December 5, 1872, crew aboard the *Dei Gratia* spotted another ship floating toward them in the Atlantic Ocean. It was clear something was wrong. When they climbed aboard it, they discovered a strangely empty ship. The 10 people who had set sail on the **Mary Celeste** from New York City a month earlier were nowhere to be found.

The Mysterious Mary Celeste

There were no signs of damage or struggle on the *Mary Celeste*. There was some water in the ship and the lifeboat was gone but it was otherwise fine for sea travel. None of the crew's belongings seemed to have been stolen and there was enough food for six months' sailing. It was as if the people on board had simply vanished into thin air.

Where Did They Go?

There are different theories about what happened. Some people believe that the crew abandoned the ship in a storm or were knocked overboard by a spinning column of water called a waterspout. Others say that pirates kidnapped them or that the crew of the *Dei Gratia* killed them all. Some suggest those aboard had been eaten by a sea monster, taken by aliens, or had disappeared due to magical forces!

The ship's name "*Mary Celeste*" has come to mean a place from which everyone has mysteriously disappeared.

Lost from a Lighthouse

In January 1900, three lighthouse keepers disappeared into the night. They were never seen or heard from again. The men had been stationed for months on the lonely island of Eilean Mor, on which no one else lived. The island is off the west coast of Scotland in the United Kingdom (UK). Joseph Moore, the man who came to replace them, said he had a bad feeling the moment he started to climb the lighthouse steps. His fears were confirmed once he entered—the men had vanished, seemingly without trace.

As If Time Stood Still

There were three unfinished meals in the kitchen and a toppled chair, as if someone had left in a hurry. The clock had stopped. It was freezing cold and the winds were bitter but one of the men's coats was still hanging in the hall. Moore and many others believed that the lighthouse keepers must have been knocked into the sea by a wave or a storm but were they?

Some lighthouses are lost and lonely places.

SPOOKED!

If the lighthouse keepers on Eilean Mor were drowned at sea, why were their bodies never washed ashore? Or if a storm had blown them off the cliffs, why had no storms been seen from nearby islands at the time? Local people avoided being on the island after dark because they said it was haunted. Lighthouse keepers reported hearing spooky moaning sounds for many years afterward.

21

The Devil's Sea

The Devil's Sea is a strange and scary area in the Pacific Ocean near Japan. Since the thirteenth century, ships and boats have been reported missing in its waters. In the late 1940s and early 1950s, a number of fishing boats and military ships vanished in the area. Many disappeared during perfect weather, when there were no dangerous storms. In 1952, a ship named *Kaiyo Maru 5* and its 31 crew vanished. In 1980, the huge *Derbyshire* ship disappeared too.

All Down to Natural Causes?

Scientists say there are **logical** explanations for the mysterious disappearances. The Devil's Sea is in an area where there are underwater volcanoes—underwater eruptions can create explosions of water and rock, as well as giant tsunami waves. Some say that methane gas beneath the ocean floor can bubble to the surface out of cracks. The gas can cause the water to froth and heave so violently that it could sink ships.

SPOOKED!

Some people remain convinced something more mysterious is happening in the Devil's Sea. There are legends of a giant dragon that once dragged ships to the bottom of the sea, and so give the area the name Dragon's Triangle.

Were the fire-breathing dragons from Japanese legend really volcanoes, or is something more spooky going on in the Devil's Sea?

What happened to the USS *Cyclops* and the many men aboard? Were they more mysterious victims of the cursed waters of the Devil's Triangle?

The Devil's Triangle

Also known as the Bermuda Triangle, the Devil's Triangle is a very spooky stretch of water that runs across the western part of the North Atlantic Ocean. Hundreds of airplanes and ships have disappeared there in mysterious, some say **supernatural**, circumstances. One of the most famous was the USS *Cyclops*, which vanished on March 4, 1918.

A Giant of the Seas

USS *Cyclops* was an enormous ship. It was built to carry thousands of tonnes of coal across the oceans, to provide fuel for steam ships while they were at sea. In 1918, during World War 1 (1914–1918), USS *Cyclops* was transporting a heavy cargo of metal from Barbados to steelworks in Baltimore for ship building. This route took the ship straight through the Devil's Triangle. *Cyclops* never made it to Baltimore.

Cyclops Goes Missing

There were 309 men on board when *Cyclops* disappeared. This is the largest non-conflict loss of life the US Navy has ever suffered. There were rumors, or stories, that the captain was very disorganized and made mistakes. Some said the load of metal was too heavy and capsized, or overturned, the ship. More than a century later, the mystery of the USS *Cyclops* remains unsolved.

THE DEEP

Spooky Seas

Out on the open seas in the middle of the ocean, it is so far from land and the gaze of curious onlookers that almost anything can happen and sometimes, it does…
In 2015, a man named Keith Davis was many thousands of miles from land when he vanished at sea. Despite many searches, his remains were never found.

Unwanted at Sea?

Keith Davis worked as a fisheries observer. Fisheries observers travel aboard the boats used to fish the world's oceans. They record how many fish are caught, whether protected fish **species** are harmed by the ships, and whether crew follow the rules made to keep the world's oceans safe. For example, fishing boats are not allowed to dump unwanted fish overboard or to catch **endangered** species. Davis spent most of his working life far from land—he lived among ships' captains and crews. Often though, these sailors felt he was there to find fault and resented him.

Gone Without a Trace

Davis joined the *Victoria 168* in August 2015 and was never seen again. He vanished hundreds of miles off the coast of Ecuador, South America in broad daylight. One minute, a crew member saw him on deck, and the next, Davis was gone. The crew searched the ship from top to bottom but found no sign of him. Another 16 boats helped scour a huge area of the ocean, trying to find Davis anywhere ocean currents might have dragged him. There was no sign of him.

Victoria 168 a was a tuna-fishing boat that set sail from Panama, South America. When the ship returned to shore a month later, Davis was not on board. What happened to him?

**Will we ever learn
what really happened to
Keith Davis that fateful day?**

What Happened?

The sea is a dangerous place. Could a wave have crashed across the deck, knocking Davis off his feet and into the water? Fishing boats are hazardous too. The heavy hooks that pull up giant nets full of fish can break free from a cable, and stab into a person. Perhaps, instead, Davis was killed by the crew that didn't want him on their ship?

Victoria 168 had large refrigerated rooms that allowed smaller boats to offload their catches at sea. This saved the smaller boats from making trips back to harbors to offload their catch. These giant fridges could also be used to hide illegal shark fin catches or drugs. Was Davis murdered to stop him reporting something that the people on *Victoria 168* didn't want him to see?

CHAPTER 4

DISAPPEARANCES IN THE SKIES

Flying is one of the safest ways to travel: When measured per mile, flying is far safer than driving or traveling by railroad. Even when airplanes are forced to land or they crash-land on water, people aboard often survive. However, there are still unsolved mysteries of planes that disappeared from the skies. No or few traces of these aircraft or the people flying in them were ever recovered.

Swallowed by the Sea?

The Devil's Triangle not only swallows up boats and ships in the sea but it also takes planes from the skies. Legends abound about this strange triangular area of ocean between Bermuda, Puerto Rico, and Miami, Florida. Scientists say that the area could be a victim of big, dangerous storms that come from different directions and meet in the area. But other people believe it has supernatural powers. Some say it's an area where aliens in spaceships kidnap planes, ships, and their crews. Some believe that the lost city of Atlantis sank to the very bottom of the ocean near here and that supernatural power from its temples is causing the losses.

Many planes are said to have vanished in the Devil's Triangle zone.

Missing in Action

On December 5, 1945, five Avenger planes on a military training mission disappeared without a trace in the Devil's Triangle area. The planes had been checked and had plenty of fuel. The pilots were experienced and the weather was fine, so why were all five planes and their crew members never found? What happened to them as they flew across the sea?

Lost in the Search

After the five planes disappeared from the ground crew's **radar**, planes and ships were sent to search for them. One of these, a seaplane, called the Mariner, with a crew of 13, also vanished from the radar. In one day, six planes had disappeared without trace in the same area.

The US Navy claimed that the Avengers' lead pilot made a mistake and led the others too far out to sea. There they ran out of fuel and crashed into stormy seas. Crew on a nearby ship said they saw a ball of fire in the sky. Could this have been the Mariner seaplane exploding in mid-air?

SPOOKED!

Something strange seemed to have happened to the Avenger planes. Radio messages showed that the planes' compasses suddenly stopped working and the weather turned stormy. One pilot said, "Everything looks strange. It looks like we're entering white water..."

The Federal Bureau of Investigation (FBI) thinks that the hijacker who jumped from a plane (see below) was a professional skydiver who died after miscalculating the winter weather and the wilderness he landed in.

SPOOKED!

Some missing planes are eventually found. *Star Dust* was an aircraft that vanished in August 1947, while flying from Argentina to Chile, South America. *Star Dust* and its 11 passengers and crew were missing for more than 50 years. Then in 1998, climbers in the Andes Mountains discovered some of the plane wreckage. In 2000, the remainder of the plane was found—along with human remains.

Dropped from the Sky

In November 1971, a man hijacked a US passenger flight. He showed flight crew a bomb in a suitcase, and demanded four parachutes and $200,000 in 20-dollar bills. Passengers were allowed to leave the plane in Seattle and the crew collected the cash and parachutes. The hijacker told the crew to fly to Mexico City. At around 8 p.m., he jumped out of the back of the plane. He was never seen again.

Deceitful or Dead?

The parachute and some of the money were later found on the banks of the Columbia River. Some people believe this suggests the hijacker did not survive the drop. Others think he could have survived but lost some of the money while jumping. Did he leave some to make it look like he died? A volcanic eruption of Mount St. Helens in 1980 likely destroyed any remaining clues about the case.

Puzzle of the Missing Plane

On March 8, 2014, Malaysia Airlines Flight 370 (MH370) was carrying 239 people when suddenly, the plane vanished from the skies. No trace of the airplane or the people aboard has been found. MH370 was flying from Malaysia to China. Ground crew were tracking its flight over the South China Sea on radar screens and noticed that the aircraft suddenly altered its planned route. There was no explanation from the pilot as to why the route was changed. And then, the plane was gone!

What Really Happened to MH370?

Search parties covered a wide area looking for MH370 but found nothing. There were no signals from beacons on the aircraft that should have sent out signals if it crashed into the ocean. Had there been a disaster so sudden that the pilots had no time to call for help? Or did one of the pilots or even hijackers cause the plane to crash on purpose? Other theories are that survivors were kidnapped when they washed ashore or that they are living on a remote island somewhere, waiting to be rescued.

The only clues ever found from MH370 are a few bits of the plane that washed up along the shores of the southern Indian Ocean in 2015 and 2016.

SPOOKY SKIES

Earhart Disappears

Amelia Earhart was an adventure-seeking pilot. In 1937, she set out to become the first person to fly around the world. Earhart never returned and neither she nor her aircraft were ever found. What happened to them?

Suddenly Gone!

Earhart and her **navigator**, Fred Noonan, planned to make several stops along their way, so they could rest and refuel. On the morning of July 2, 1937, they left New Guinea, an island in the Pacific Ocean, on one of the last legs in their trip. They headed for Howland Island, about 2,500 miles (4,023 km) away. A United States Coast Guard boat called the *Itasca* was waiting at Howland Island, ready to guide Earhart to the island. At some point, she lost radio contact with the *Itasca*. Then, Earhart simply disappeared.

A Search in Vain

The US government sent 9 ships, 4,000 people, and 66 aircraft to find Earhart. For 16 days, they searched a wide area of sea and remote islands. But, despite all of this, nothing was found.

Crashed and Died or Crashed and Survived?

In the years after her disappearance, there were many theories about what happened to Earhart. Officials said Earhart ran out of fuel and in the cloudy weather, lost her way and crashed into the sea. Yet, radio operators in the United States and across the Pacific reported receiving messages from Earhart or strange sounds that could have been sent by her. In the 1940s, there were reports of people seeing Earhart in New Jersey, where she was living under a new name. Some people believe she made it to a island where she starved to death.

HAMMOND - Y

Earhart already had several record-breaking flights under her belt. Why did she so easily disappear?

After Earhart's plane disappeared, bones were found on a Pacific island, Nikumaroro. The find was recorded, but soon after, the bones disappeared. Some people believe they may have belonged to Earhart...

The Mystery Continues

Earhart vanished during a time of growing tension between Japan and the United States, just before World War II (1939–1945). There were claims that Earhart was on a spy mission for the United States and that is why the US government might have covered up the truth about her disappearance. Perhaps she was captured and killed by Japanese forces? We may never know.

CHAPTER 5

THE HILLS HOLD LIES

Remote mountains and hills can be wild and lonely places. They can be covered in thick, dark forests, and bleak, rocky slopes that are blasted by fierce winds. It is not unusual for hikers who are unprepared for the weather conditions or the physical demands of a climb to die on mountains. However, many hills and mountains have been the center of some spooky unexplained disappearances. Were these curious vanishings caused by violent nature, dangerous people, or something more otherworldy?

Missing Persons

An area of southwestern Vermont became known as the Bennington Triangle after it was the center of a series of spine-chilling missing persons' cases. Native American legends say that the area is cursed. One legend tells of a mysterious stone in the mountains that opens up and swallows anyone foolish enough to step on it. Others tell of hairy half-men roaming the land.

A Dark Secret

The Bennington Triangle holds a dark secret. It is here that five people disappeared between 1945 and 1950. In November 1945, hunting guide Middie Rivers disappeared. In December 1946, Paula Jean Welden vanished after telling her roommate she was going for a walk. Three years later, James Tedford was on a bus to Bennington but had disappeared when the bus arrived. Spookily, his belongings were still in the luggage rack. Schoolboy Paul Jepson disappeared from the back of a truck in 1950, and that same year, experienced hiker Frieda Langer also vanished.

SPOOKED!

Bigfoot is a legendary creature reportedly sighted across North America. It got its name from the massive footprints it is said to leave behind. The legend of Bigfoot likely comes from the Native American **myth** of large, hairy humanlike creatures named Sasquatches. However, Bigfoot creatures are generally believed to warn people of danger, rather than be a danger to people themselves.

Hidden mine shafts, a dangerous serial killer, a ferocious animal, or supernatural forces? These are all possible explanations for the mysterious disappearances in the Bennington Triangle.

Murder or Mystery?

Some say bad weather or old, unmarked mine shafts caused some of the disappearances. Others believe a murderer or mountain lion killed the people who disappeared. Many are still convinced strange forces were at work. There were also reports of terrifying voices calling out on radios, sightings of mysterious figures, and odd, unexplained problems with navigation tools.

The Mountain That Swallows People

Mount Nyangani in Zimbabwe, southern Africa, has been linked to legends for centuries, earning it the nickname "The Mountain That Swallows People." Powerful, evil spirits and other supernatural creatures are said to live there, some of whom enjoy pushing people from steep ledges. Many have disappeared on the spooky mountain over the decades.

Strange Events

Mount Nyangani is a place where strange things have been reported. Compasses and other electrical equipment suddenly break and photos taken do not print.

People feel dizzy, confused, and lost for no reason. Strange sounds have been heard and groups of animals watch and follow people around. Sometimes, gusts of wind and thick fog or mist appear out of nowhere and seem to stalk hikers.

Lost Lives

In 1981, two teenage girls vanished from Mount Nyangani without a trace. Not even a huge air and ground search could find them. A few years later, a 12-year-old boy wandered off during a school field trip and vanished. In 2014, a 31-year-old man went on a hike and vanished… These are just some of the most recent cases but many others have been reported too.

Why are some mountains the site of mysterious disappearances?

A Black and Bleak Mountain

Black Mountain in Queensland, Australia, is a place of mystery and legend. Since the late 1800s, this mass of huge, dark granite boulders has been famed for stories of people disappearing. Couriers, criminals, and cattle herders have all been lost here. People looking for gold, explorers, and hikers have all vanished.

Eerie Echoes

Scientists say they can explain the mysterious disappearances and the strange sounds that echo through the mountain. They believe that wind blowing through the boulders makes sounds that could be mistaken for howling souls trapped inside. They insist that explosive and tumbling noises happen when the granite boulders crack because of weathering, or being worn away by rain or wind. They also say that the boulders have big gaps, and that climbing them is dangerous. People could easily slip into the gaps and disappear.

SPOOKED!

The **indigenous** owners of the mountain call it "Kalkajaka," which means place of spear. They say it was a **sacred** battlefield and the location of an important spear fight between two groups that were fighting over hunting grounds. They say many warriors died and were buried in the mountains. For many indigenous people, it is a sacred site where no one is allowed to go. If they do, they risk getting very, very sick.

MOODY MOUNTAINS

Spooky Mountains

As its name suggests, the Superstition Mountain range in Arizona is a strange and spooky place. The area is said to be filled with ghost stories, mysterious lights in the sky, screams, and shadows. Some people believe that there are supernatural forces there that people do not understand. It is true that there have been many unexplained and mysterious disappearances in this mountain range.

The Superstition Mountains have steep volcanic peaks and ridges, and boulder-filled canyons. There are dangerous cliffs and deadly desert regions that suffer scorching temperatures and have few sources of water.

Highway to Hell?

In the past, Native American Apaches believed there was a hole in these mountains that led straight into an underworld, or Hell. According to local stories, wind blowing out of this hole causes the many severe dust storms that happen in the area and that can make it difficult for people to see where they are going. Certainly it is a place where hellish things happen. There have been stories of people being injured by or narrowly escaping large boulders that suddenly hurtle toward them, as if someone or something had pushed them.

Bodies with gruesome gunshot wounds have been buried in the mountains. Sometimes, only skulls are discovered...

Cursed Treasure Hunt?

Many people have disappeared in the Superstitions while searching for the Lost Dutchman's Gold Mine. This vast legendary area of gold is said to have a deadly curse on it. Some stories say the valuable mine belonged to a long-lost Native American Apache tribe. Later it was found but lost again by a Dutch or German treasure hunter, from whom it takes its name.

Another Victim

Treasure hunter Adolph Ruth set off to make his fortune in 1931 but he never returned. His skull was later found in one place and the rest of his remains were found even later, elsewhere. Did Ruth die from heat exhaustion and wild animals carried his body away in parts? Or was he another victim of the curse of the Superstitions?

Missing, Believed Dead

Some say as many as 600 people have died searching for Lost Dutchman's Gold Mine, and many have gone missing. On July 11, 2010, three hikers from Utah went missing in the Superstitions while looking for the mine. In January 2011, three sets of remains, assumed to be those of the lost men, were discovered.

CHAPTER 6

LOST CITIES AND COMMUNITIES

The idea of an entire village, town, or kingdom vanishing without a trace is one of the most chilling mysteries imaginable. These are cases of not just one or a few people going missing but stories of whole communities disappearing. Sometimes, people start to believe these communities never existed but then suddenly, a discovery reveals the **tragedy** of people simply lost in time.

A Lost City

Dvãrakã was said to be an ancient city on the coast of India. Legend says that in the city, there were 900,000 royal palaces, built of crystal and silver and decorated with huge emeralds. Until the twentieth century, many people thought Dvãrakã was a myth. Then, in 1963, **archeologists** found evidence that there had been an ancient settlement on the site of present-day Dwarka. They also discovered stone blocks and pillars from ancient walls deep beneath the sea. Could these be evidence that the city of Dvãrakã existed?

True or False?

In 1939, a Canadian fur trapper named Joe Labelle arrived in an Inuit village called Anjikuni, where he often stopped. The village was strangely empty. Everything was just as if the hundreds of villagers who had lived there had vanished into thin air. Their boats, hunting rifles, and food were all waiting but no one was to be found. Investigators found no trace of the villagers and later it was suggested that Labelle had never visited the village before. Was it all just a creepy hoax? What really happened in Anjikuni remains a strange and unsolved mystery.

What really happened
on that full moon
winter night before
Joe Labelle arrived in
the Inuit village
of Anjikuni?

SPOOKED!

There were other unsolved mysteries
about Anjikuni. Inuit people from
nearby villages reported seeing
strange blue lights in the sky.
Investigators may have found no
villagers at the scene but they did
discover the bodies of seven sled dogs
still tied to their posts. It appeared
that they had starved to death.
Inuit people relied on dogs to pull
the sleds on which they traveled
and it is unthinkable that they
left the dogs behind.

Overwhelmed by the Ocean

The Lost City of Atlantis is one of the oldest mysteries of the world. This ancient city full of gold, silver, and other treasures is said to have vanished in a day. One legend tells that the people of Atlantis became rich through war and angered Zeus, king of the Greek gods. He punished them by sending earthquakes and floods that sank Atlantis beneath the ocean. Another legend says that Atlantis was destroyed by floods created when a comet crashed on Earth.

Atlantis Found?

The story of Atlantis captured people's imaginations for years but there was no evidence that the city ever existed. Then in 2011, archeologists using **satellite** imagery and radar that can reach underground, found Atlantis, or at least a city that could be Atlantis. The city was buried beneath swampy land north of Cádiz in southern Spain. The remains of the city have yet to be investigated, but could it perhaps be Atlantis?

SPOOKED!

Some stories claim that the people who originally lived in Atlantis were aliens who arrived there about 50,000 years ago from space. These aliens were very tall and fair, and lived for up to 800 years. There are even stories that they could control the weather and volcanic eruptions.

Did the city of Atlantis exist 10,000 years ago and was it lost when earthquakes and floods destroyed it?

Was Troy burned down by enemy Greek soldiers?

A Doomed City

The story of the Trojan War has fascinated people for thousands of years. The war is said to have been fought between the ancient cities of Troy and Greek Sparta. It started when a prince of Troy kidnapped the wife of the king of Sparta. Greek soldiers tricked the Trojans by hiding inside a huge wooden horse, called the Trojan Horse. When the Trojans allowed the wooden horse inside the city, the Greeks leaped out of it and defeated Troy. After this, the city seems to have disappeared.

Lost in Time

Many people have searched for the city of Troy. In 1871, German archeologist Heinrich Schliemann discovered the location of ruins that could be Troy in what is now Turkey. The ruins are clearly of a city preparing for war. There are high walls and **trenches** built to store **chariots** that could be ridden into battle. Some of the remains show signs of an attack from an enemy, with stones scorched by fire. Does this suggest Troy and its people were wiped out by Greek armies in the thirteenth century BCE?

The Search for Himiko's Home

The legendary kingdom of Yamatai in Japan, and its most famous ruler Queen Himiko, are surrounded in mystery. Himiko was said to have been a **shaman** who controlled the kingdom using magical powers to make the people of Yamatai choose her to rule them. Himiko lived in a towered fortress guarded by 100 men. Inside, she was waited on by 1,000 female servants. When Himiko died in CE 248, it is said 100 slaves were killed in her honor.

Tomb Raiders

In 2009, archeologists believed they found Himiko's tomb, and that could mean they had also found the missing city. In 2015, investigations of the tomb revealed a burned boar bone and more than 100 frog bones. These could have been used in **rituals**: Burning animal bones is known to have been used to tell the future. The discovery of a special mirror in the tomb that may have been used for magic, suggests to some that Himiko's kingdom of Yamatai was located in this area.

One theory as to what caused Thonis-Heracleion to disappear is that a violent earthquake suddenly turned the clay upon which the city was built to liquid. Within moments, this ancient wonder sank into a muddy tomb and was gradually buried deeper and deeper by layer upon layer of sand.

In the early 2000s, a group of divers working off the Egyptian coast found the salt-covered remains of the statue of the god Hapy, and of the lost city of Thonis-Heracleion.

The City Beneath the Sea

Imagine swimming through murky waters far below the ocean's surface and suddenly coming upon a large and stern, stony face, staring out into the gloom. This is how divers discovered remains of the god Hapy and finally solved the mystery of the missing ancient Egyptian city of Thonis-Heracleion.

Secrets of a City

Thonis-Heracleion had been a bustling and important trading port around 2,700 years ago. There would have been boats all around it, and people buying and selling things such as perfume, **papyrus**, and silver. Then, one day, the ground below their feet suddenly gave way. The city and the people in it disappeared completely under water. Modern-day divers are using huge underwater vacuum cleaners to suck up layers of land to uncover the city's secret.

THE LOST COLONY

Spooky Settlers

How could more than 100 men, women, and children just disappear? This is a question that has haunted people for hundreds of years. The lost **colony** of Roanoke is one of the most famous unsolved mysteries in US history. Roanoke, in what is now North Carolina, would have been the first permanent English colony in North America in 1587 if everyone there had not suddenly and mysteriously vanished.

Disappeared into the Darkness

John White, the mayor of Roanoke, left the colony in its first year. White returned to England to get supplies and more settlers to help build a successful colony. His trip back was delayed and when he finally arrived back in Roanoke three years later, there was no one at the coast to greet him. The settlement was empty. Everyone in it—his wife, child, and grandchild, and all of the other settlers—had vanished into thin air.

Were the Roanoke settlers victims of a Native American attack or is there another reason for their disappearance?

What was behind the mysterious carving of the word CROATOAN that White found when he revisited the colony?

Murder Mystery

White's first thought was that the people in the colony had been murdered by Native Americans who feared settlers, some of whom had brought death and disease. But there were no signs that buildings had been burned and there were no human remains. So, he assumed there must be another explanation for the mysterious disappearance of the settlers.

Clues in the Colony?

The only clue White found was the word CROATOAN carved into fencing. The Croatoan Native American tribe lived on an island about 60 miles (97 km) south. Unfortunately, a hurricane stopped White reaching the island. He decided to spend winter in the Caribbean and continue his search in the spring but his ship was blown off course and he headed back to England.

Murdered or Died?

In 1603, a search expedition tried to find the colonists but it was forced back by bad weather and threats from indigenous peoples. The lack of hard evidence led to different theories about what happened. Did the colonists try to sail back to England and die at sea? Perhaps the settlers died of disease or starvation. Or maybe, after all, they were killed by indigenous people.

Silenced Forever?

An outline of two forts hidden in invisible ink was found on an old map White made. Did the colonists move to one of these secret locations? Or maybe they moved in with the friendly Croatoan tribe? The mysterious thing is, if the colonists survived and found a new place to live, why did they not let people know where they were? To this day no one knows what became of the settlers, and it remains one of history's great unsolved mysteries.

GLOSSARY

Aboriginal the first people to live in a country

archeologists people who study history through artifacts and remains

chariots two-wheeled vehicles drawn by horses

colony a group of people who settle in a new place

currents large areas of air or water moving in a certain direction

DNA the substance in cells that carries unique information about living things

empire a group of countries or regions that are controlled by one ruler or one government

endangered at risk of dying out or becoming extinct

expeditions organized journeys for a particular purpose

headland a narrow strip of land that sticks out from a coast into the sea

hijacker a person who illegally takes control of something such as an airplane

historian someone who studies the past

indigenous existing in a land from the earliest times

Inuit the indigenous peoples of Arctic North America

legend a traditional story

logical reasonable and sensible

marrow the soft substance that fills the hollow parts of bones

mummies bodies that have been preserved

mummified preserved a dead body as a mummy

myth traditional story that explains a natural event

navigator person who plans or controls where a vehicle is going

papyrus a paper-like material made from plants in ancient Egypt

pneumonia a lung disease

radar a system that uses radio waves to locate objects

ransom a sum of money demanded or paid for the release of a captive or hostage

rebels people who fight against their government or rulers

remote far away

rituals actions performed in a certain way, especially as part of a religious ceremony

rustler a person who rounds up and steals cattle, horses, or sheep

sacred holy or connected to the gods

sandbar a long, narrow bank of sand

satellite an electronic device placed in orbit around Earth

shaman a person believed to have powers to heal the sick

species a type of living thing

supernatural a force for which there is no scientific explanation

tragedy an event that causes great suffering, destruction, and distress

trenches narrow holes dug into the ground

tsar an emperor (leader) of Russia before 1917

FIND OUT MORE

Books

Gagliardi, Sue. *Amelia Earhart* (Unsolved Mysteries).
North Star Editions, 2023.

Harder, Megan. *Inside the Bermuda Triangle* (Top Secret).
Lerner Publications, 2023.

Jaznyka, Kitson. *History's Mysteries: Freaky Phenomena: Curious Clues, Cold Cases, and Puzzles from the Past.* National Geographic Kids, 2018.

McCarthy, Tom. *Weird Disappearances: Real Tales of Missing People* (Mystery and Mayhem). Nomad Press, 2017.

Websites

Read about some more mysterious disappearances at:
www.britannica.com/list/9-mysterious-disappearances-of-people-other-than-amelia-earhart

Learn more about Henry Hudson at:
https://exploration.marinersmuseum.org/subject/henry-hudson

Find out more about the Bermuda Triangle at
www.wonderopolis.org/wonder/how-big-is-the-bermuda-triangle

Publisher's note to educators and parents:
All the websites featured above have been carefully reviewed to ensure that they are suitable for students. However, many websites change often, and we cannot guarantee that a site's future contents will continue to meet our high standards of educational value. Please be advised that students should be closely monitored whenever they access the Internet.

INDEX

About the Author

Louise Spilsbury is an award-winning children's book author. She has written countless books about history and science. In writing and researching this book, she is more spooked than ever by mysterious disappearances!